The book is dedicated to the thousands of clients we've served over the years in appreciation for their efforts and for paying my price. I'd also like to thank my lovely fiancé who designed the cover of this book as a means to stimulate me to write it. I'd also like to thank my children who not only allowed me the freedom to write, they actually read some of the book on their Kindles.

PRICING YOUR PRACTICE

The Mindset To Get Paid What You Are Worth

Eric David Greenspan

Copyright © 2018 Eric Greenspan

All rights reserved.

CHAPTER ONE
Introduction

Why I Wrote It

Pricing Your Practice is a guide to help you build your pricing, sell it and achieve great success. It's also about strength and courage, building your confidence, establishing your value, learning to believe in it and yourself, and most importantly, learn how to sell what you're worth. Finally, this book will help you face reality and to make sure you are being paid properly, earning enough, and living the life you've worked so hard to achieve and deserve.

Pricing is very difficult for so many, at least from our experience working with professionals in the accounting and bookkeeping industry. They often question their ability, and of course confidence plays a major role here. But beyond that, it's just a cumbersome proposition. Sure, you can copy the competitor down the hall, but is that what you really want to do? Wouldn't you rather establish pricing that has reason, something you believe in, and one that you can sell with great confidence? I know I do and that is part of the reason I wrote this book.

Another reason I wrote this book is because I knew it would be useful for a large audience. We did the research and our stats show that pricing is one of the most popular and attended event topic at schoolofbookkeeping.com and schooloftaxes.com. It became clear that this is where we were needed. If you want to sell a lot of books, sell books people want to read!

Finally, I wrote this book because my soon to be wife designed the cover, sent it to my inbox and said, "write this." So I did. Ironically, she set it in my mind. Mindset. Hmmmm. You might hear about that again as you read on.

The Importance of Pricing

Pricing is important. Getting pricing right in the beginning is critical and managing pricing over time must not be overlooked. Pricing is not static, because life is not static. The only certainty in life besides death and taxes are rising costs. Remember when you could play a video game for a quarter or make a phone call for a dime? Ya, it's a bit fuzzy to me too. But we can likely agree that everything generally goes up in price, from a gallon of milk, to a plane ticket, to filing a tax return. And yes, there are corrections, and it all comes crashing down, but it never seems to stay down and it always seems to reach new highs before the next crash. I just want you to make sure you remember your part in the cycle. You have to buy the milk and the plane ticket at the higher price and the only way you can do this is by charging more for your services. It's just simple math.

Over time, you will get better at doing what you do, and the best, earn more, or at least they should. Many of our clients complain that they are working harder and earning the same. They often speak of clients that require more hand holding, and almost always, those clients are the ones that pay the least. This is unhealthy, degrading, and over time, can cause great stress and lead to financial hardship. In the end, if you don't properly price yourself, properly change and adapt your pricing, you will find a slippery slope on the way to financial awfulness, and once you are on it, it takes a lot to get back on to solid ground.

Often, when we get started we price ourselves at a level that we feel we can sell, usually lower than we like. Over time, we get busy and we increase our pricing for new clients a little here and there, but we get stuck in our ways and sometimes, we just forget. Maybe we're getting lazy. Maybe we don't remember. Maybe we have too many other things on our minds. Our pricing seems to be working. We're busy as can be. We find it easy to sell our services at this level we've set, so we get complacent and we just let another day pass, and another, and another. Eventually, we focus on other parts of our business and we forget to revisit the issue. Well, don't forget, ever. Pricing is important.

The business continues to grow; we are making money. Life's good. Meanwhile, if our customers all got in a room together and discussed their relationship with us, the one thing they'd all say in common is, "Working with [firm name] is a joy and a GREAT BARGAIN." I like that they think of us positively but a great bargain, I never want to be that to anyone. Life's too short and I've worked too hard. This is what I call Pricing Perception and it has two sides. We'll talk about that more in a later chapter.

Pricing can keep us from reaching our potential. It holds us back, and we fear raising our prices as that would require more sales effort, create a longer sales cycle, or even allow us to lose potential customers that just don't see the value. As entrepreneurs, we took this on as part of the challenge of being a business owner, so if you want your business to be a success, you have to look it in the face and own it.

Pricing requires us to make choices about who we are and our value. Either we price ourselves too low, or we lack the confidence or faith in our abilities, or we lack the skills required to close a sale based on our value, rather than the idea of a "great deal." I for one fear the "great deal" offered by service providers. Anyone who sells themselves short, probably lacks the confidence to get the job done as well. I once asked a client, "What would you charge me to do my taxes?" The response was so low, I found someone else.

CHAPTER TWO
Who Am I?

EDG

My name is Eric David Greenspan. If you follow me on social media, you already know that I have ferocious passion for marketing, technology, workflow and automation. I'm also a father, a husband, a soccer coach, and a hockey dad. I love all these things.

I also love to help accounting professionals grow and manage their practice. I do this in my day job at 74 Systems where we run the Ignite Program for accountants, bookkeepers, and business owners. We also run two online educational resources: schoolofbookkeeping.com and schooloftaxes.com as well as our beloved ABBO on Facebook.

I also created the Percentage Pricing model. You can learn about that on schoolofbookkeeping.com. There's a couple of recorded WOWbinars on the topic and you can download the template to use for your pricing strategy.

Oh and one other thing…I'm not the chef Eric Greenspan from Food Network. While I do love to cook, and I have met him, we're not the same guy. We both also know the lawyer Eric Greenspan, but he doesn't get a lot of social media airtime, so rarely do we cross paths. Ironically, someone emailed me today asking questions about my new restaurant. Wrong EG.

I'm a marketer, a business builder, a techie, a hockey dad and I work with accounting and bookkeeping professionals. It's really that simple. Who are you?

Visit me at:

ericgreenspan.com

The Ignite Program

After great success and a big flop, I found myself looking for the next thing in my career. I stumbled upon schoolofbookkeeping.com (SOB) and built it into a leading provider of education tools and resources for bookkeepers and business owners.

SOB was built by 74 Systems, my company. The company was originally formed as 74 Marketing. We were very successful in helping our clients find and close new customers for their practices. So successful, that one day one of our clients called and said, "You know Eric, you really made a mess out of things. I'm so busy now because of you! I need help managing it!" And then it hit me…while marketing is my strong suit, the other thing I'm really good at is workflow and automation, namely operational management. So we converted the fast growing 74 Marketing into 74 Systems. We went from being merely a marketing consulting firm to offering marketing, technology, workflow and automation services. Boom, we took off!

Recently, we launched schooloftaxes.com, specifically for CPAs, EAs, and other tax professionals to use a set of education tools and resources for igniting their practice.

Our online "schools" offer WOWbinars™, Live [Demo] Courses, complete courses for instructional learning of basic principles and applications, plus a variety of other learning materials, templates and tools.

74 Systems works directly with our clients to help them build their practice. We become their marketing department, IT, and co-CEO when applicable. Our experience runs deep, so it's the perfect fit for us.

Pricing Your Practice

Visit us at:

74systems.com

schoolofbookkeeping.com

schooloftaxes.com

facebook.com/groups/AccountantsBookkeepersBusiness

CHAPTER THREE
What Are You Worth?

Briana, CPA

Briana is a client, a great client. We are doing great things together. Why? Because she's smart and follows through. She's also kind, reasonable, and appreciative of our help. But what makes Briana such a slam dunk success is her confidence and superb ability to think on her feet, and when she doesn't know the answer, she finds it. There's absolutely nothing wrong with saying, "I haven't a clue, but give me a couple of hours and I'll get you the right answer." It actually makes you look smarter. The truth is none of us know it all, and all of us must continue learning. There's a huge difference between stupidity and ignorance. Stupid is something you're born with. Ignorance is something you choose. Briana is smart, but she's also unwilling to allow herself to be ignorant.

One day Briana, or Bree as she likes to be called by people in her "circle," decided to get her CPA license. No small feat, that is for sure. But beyond that, Briana got a job. When she was hired, her former employer said, "Where do you see yourself in 5 years?" Her response, "I want to own your company." She did it in less than 4 years. Confidence, commitment, follow through, intellect and willingness to do what it takes to get things done. She negotiated the deal, got a big SBA loan, and bought the 35 year old company. She literally hit the ground running the next day. I mean seriously, how cool is that story?

In her first year, Briana had her work cut out for her. Many of the clients were curious about the change, some unhappy about it. While she had been at this firm she now acquired for over 4 years, it was her first year on her own. She needed support. So she hired me (74 Systems - Ignite Program).

The first thing I told her to do is hire others. She did.

Then, we built systems, processes, made sure everyone was doing their work, and she delivered on her commitments. Did it go flawlessly? Nah, but she nailed it.

Over the year, we discussed her rates. We raised her rates. Briana is paying her big loan to the SBA on time each month, making payroll, and covering her overhead.

Now, we are working on making Bree and her firm a big name in the industry. Next season, we plan to grow at a solid rate, continuing to enhance and refine systems and processes, and seek new clients nationwide. We built Books With Beers, Bree's partner program. She passes bookkeeping services to her partners; they pass tax work back. The synergy between Bree keeps growing, so does her partner list. Bree's personality has enabled this, but also her hard work and dedication has seen it through. Again, it's confidence you'll sense if you become a partner. Bree is good at her job, so offering services to Bree's referrals is a no brainer. She's not questioning her abilities. Her biggest challenge will be hiring more staff. Ironically, this may be her strongest skill.

Confidence Scale

The Confidence Scale (CS) is a tool we use to determine where you stand in comparison to your competition and to determine your CS#. We use a standard 1 to 10 scale, where 10 is the highest. As a percentage, we simply divide the number you believe fits you by 10.

To determine your CS#, find someone in the industry you'd give a 10, without question. I'm talking about a rainmaker, the one with all the certifications, degrees, nicest offices, and highest prices. I know a few of these. Sadly, they aren't as good as they think. But the point is to find someone who at least thinks they are the leader, and behaves, from a pricing perspective, accordingly. It doesn't matter if they suck, it only matters if they can sell themselves and people are buying. If you have trouble finding someone to compare yourself to, ask a friend or colleague. I'm pretty sure a quick Google Search can get you what you're looking for, but if you are still stuck, book a consult with us 74systems.com/start.

Once you find someone to compare to, compare yourself in skills and pricing, but focus more on their pricing, and your skills. Are you less skilled? Are they higher priced? Be honest with yourself here and be a tough grader. If you are much alike, then you are a 10 too. If you are close but they charge 20% more, give yourself an 8. Not even close, give yourself a 1, 2 or 3.

If you gave yourself a 10, consider looking deeper for a more experienced and higher priced competitor. If you can't, you're probably doing just fine.

If you gave yourself anything less than 10, you now can start the process of building your confidence and the good news is by reading this book, you are already working on it. Well done.

Determining Your Worth (Value)

We just gave you a great example of a leader in the industry who has tremendous confidence and what that allowed her to achieve. Now let's turn the lens towards you.

Assuming you've used the prior Confidence Scale and determined your CS#, or at least have a ballpark view in your mind of where you stand in the mix, you can now start to focus on value perception. In terms of value, we are specifically referring to your value as a provider of services and more specifically how that effects and relates to your price.

The perception of value is based on many things, including training, skills, and ability. You could probably throw in passion and intellect too, but more than any of those aforementioned, value is often tied most closely to your level of confidence.

While a standard formula to calculate value most likely does not exist (at least for this application), I suppose you could make one and it would look a little like this:

Assumptions: Demand exists, demographics accounted for in competitor pricing.

(Competitor pricing) + Your Skills (CS# / 10) = Your Value

The formula above is math, based on perception. I really love sharing the

Pricing Your Practice

CS# idea, as it really helps us align ourselves in an industry. But we really can't determine your value using a formula, because while we calculated your CS# to determine your relative level of confidence, what we don't know is why you lack confidence or what we need to do to fix it. Not yet, anyhow.

In reality, your value is a perception, both yours and that of your clients. So now let's see if we can figure out where you lack confidence and what to do to fix it.

CHAPTER FOUR
Achieving Confidence

Confidence is a Mindset

There are many factors that will lead you to success, but without confidence in your abilities or the belief in yourself to achieve your goals, you will struggle. Confidence improvement is something you desire, and if it's not innate, you will need to find it and/or create it. To do so, confidence improvement must become your mindset. You must be passionate about anything you wish to achieve. This is what success is all about. Many wealthy individuals had to overcome a weakness. Lack of confidence is just another hurdle on the track to success. Conquer it, raise your prices, thrive. But to do so, you must set your mind to it and remain focused. Life is short, get on it!

As a kid, I remember mom saying, "If you want it bad enough, you'll get it." What mom meant was "If you put your mind to it, it will happen." She was telling me to set my mind to see what I wanted and then work hard to make it happen. This setting of the mind, or your mindset, is the difference between achievement and lack thereof. For now, if you lack it confidence, make it your mindset.

It makes me think of my kids. When they want dessert, it usually begins with a couple of hints. "Dad, I ate all my vegetables. Can I have yours?" To which I reply, "Sure son, but you still cannot have dessert." To which he replies, almost always, "Oh dad, I wasn't asking for dessert." This little game happens often and eventually I'll hear, "Dad, I've been really good, can I please, please, please have a little tiny dessert? Please dad? You are so handsome and smart. Have you lost weight?" The kid has his mind set on dessert. Ok, so maybe its actually an obsession, but the most successful people in the world would argue that what they wanted was very similar to my son's desire for dessert.

If you have trouble getting your mind set on building your confidence, or building your business for that matter, perhaps you are in the wrong business. If you are not passionate about what you do, do something else. For now, I'll assume you have the mindset to build your confidence, raise your prices, sell high priced services, and build a successful and thriving practice and life. Is your mind set?

Why We Lack Confidence and What to Do About It

My all time favorite movie is *A Few Good Men* with Tom Cruise. I think much of my vocabulary is a cross between him and Eddie Murphy standup. When my family watches *Raw* or *Delirious* with me, and for sure *A Few Good Men*, they are sure to glance over at me as if to say "ha, now I know why you say that."

One of my favorite sayings from *A Few Good Men* is when Kaffee (Tom Cruise) is asked by Galloway (Demi Moore) to fight in court for the accused. Kaffee responds, "It doesn't matter what I believe. It only matters what I can prove! So please, don't tell me what I know, or don't know; I know the law." It wreaks of confidence; perhaps that's why I love it so much. But if we were to rework this for our purposes, we'd say the following:

"It doesn't matter what I believe I'm worth or my prices should be. It only matters what I can sell!

Confidence! We cannot sell what we do not believe. Even if we believe, we may not believe enough. Discounting is not a bad thing, but discounting because your customers won't buy, is a very bad thing. Assuming what you are selling is valid and in high demand, and that your pricing is in line with the industry, the only factor behind why you are not selling or in this case, "closing," is because you don't properly believe in your ability, your product/service and yourself.

I've always been on a stage, in front of people, leading a group or company, and yet, I'm terrified of it all. In school, I never raised my hand and hid behind the kid in front of me. I was sure to never make eye contact with my teacher in fear she might call on me. I used to have nightmares that I would be called on and my class would make fun of me. I mean who hasn't had the occasional "forgot to put clothes on before I left for school" dream right? But for me, it was worse. On days when I knew I had to present in front of a class, I'd pray to wake up with Chicken Pox or for a natural disaster. I'd tell myself that "everyone has to do this Eric" but that didn't really help much. I was just plain scared. I lacked confidence. Had I known then, what I know… oh never mind…you get the point.

I moved to Santa Barbara in 1987, after a year in College at Kent State University in Ohio. I had grown up in Palm Springs, California, and sent to Ohio for High School. I was excited to get back to SoCal. When I arrived, I enrolled at the local city college; what a gorgeous and great school it was and remains to be today.

One day in the bookstore, I applied for the Nellie Mae Loan for Learning to buy an IBM PS/2 Model 55sx computer. I got the loan and the computer. I was so excited and spent hours playing around on this thing. I had a friend that had tons of software from his job, and he shared it all with me. I was in heaven. There where floppy disks EVERYWHERE!

In a few days, I managed to mess up the operating system pretty badly and called for help. Somehow, I got routed to the local IBM office and the guy who helped me spent hours on the phone explaining how to install DOS and Windows 3.0. The next day I went back into the bookstore with my new knowledge and passion for computers and helped the IBM rep sell another family. He was so appreciative, he offered me an internship with IBM. I had to meet with someone at the local IBM office to seal the deal. I was so nervous. When I arrived, I sat in a room alone in my only dress shirt, no tie. In walks a man in a white shirt and a tie, status quo for IBM, and introduced himself. I smiled and said, "aren't you the guy that helped me on the phone for hours the other day?" He said, "ha, that was you?" I got the gig. My confidence from learning how to install DOS and Windows led me to an internship with IBM, which increased my confidence and later I was offered full time employment with IBM. My confidence just kept on rising and in 1996, I started my own computer tech company. I now had a CS# nearing 10, maybe even higher, which we will discuss shortly.

Later in my career, and at my 3rd startup, I was raising money with a group

Pricing Your Practice

in Southern California for another tech services business I created. I had to do a pitch to 125 investors. I was behind a podium and I for one do not like podiums. I like to pace or sit on a desk. But today, I had a podium and I could not have been happier about it! As I stood at the podium about to present aka "pitch", my leg was shaking and I mean really shaking. I was sure they knew but at least I had the podium. Then, I started to warm up and get into my groove. You see, I loved my role, my company and I truly believed in it. So, after a few minutes, my leg stopped shaking and started to soar. We landed the largest investment from that group in history at the time and as the commitments started to flow in, my legs shook less and less at future pitches. In the end, my confidence grew, as I achieved my goals.

Achieving confidence comes from many things. It might be your skills and knowledge. It might be the amount of time you've spent doing what you do. It might be innate. And it almost always increases from achievement in life and the success of your business.

A great way to achieve confidence is to set goals, obtainable goals, and then obtain them. Then, set new goals, but raise the bar a little higher each time. As you progress, you will grow your confidence and you'll look back and wonder how you ever felt like you once did.

I've been to TED (twice) and I ran TEDxAmericanRiviera in Santa Barbara for a couple of years with some colleagues. At TED, I lacked confidence. I mean seriously, sitting with 2,500 of the smartest people in the world? Ya, no idea how I got in, but I just kept quiet and listened. I made a ton of new friends and that helped a little, but usually got lost in the discussions. I'll never forget watching a man rap lyrics about quantum physics in a hot tub with an acoustic guitar sporting a killer afro and a huge smile to boot. At TEDxAR, also a smart bunch, but here I fit in a little better. Since it was my event, I was on stage in front of hundreds several times, there was no podium, and my legs didn't shake a bit. Over time, you grow confidence and things just get easier. Be patient, work hard, do, and your confidence will build.

Confidence vs. Cocky

Earlier I shared an anecdote about my life and achieving confidence. While most things we believe to be true about ourselves are based on perception, it was likely that the perception of me at that time in my career was either "wow, that guy is sexy…" which means I had confidence and that is often deemed sexy (think Jack Nicholson). Or, perhaps, what they were saying is "this guy is over the top. He's beyond confident. He's just plain cocky." I'm confident enough today to admit that I was over-confident aka cocky, back then. Avoid this, it will not serve you well.

When I started my second company, after selling my first, and receiving a large capital investment, I booked an airline ticket for a meeting in NYC for myself and for our Chairman. When I was on the phone with United, he said, "Book first class. We're in the big leagues now. From this day forward, you will always fly first class." From that day on, I started thinking of myself differently. The good news was it helped me close deals and grow the company. But it got the better of me. I left the company and sold my shares and rebooted. I love first class, but I needed to fix a few things and so I did.

I've worked with a ton of professionals in the accounting industry. I've helped build their "brands" including their personal one. Often, the stage and fans and newly found attention, to someone that has never really been "popular," can lead them towards a patch of destruction. I won't go into details, but if things start rocking for you, keep yourself in check.

It's important to make sure you don't allow yourself to become cocky. Confidence is a great thing to have, but if overdone, it can lead to disaster. Strive for confidence and never give up. When you get there, make sure to check yourself once in a while make sure you're not over-the-top or becoming cocky. If you are, fix it, and fix it fast.

10 Steps to Achieving Confidence

Here are ten things you can do to help you achieve higher confidence

1. Set achievable goals daily. Achieve them. Set new ones and keep going.

2. Make sure you always deliver on your promises. It's very important to do what you say you're going to do. It's better to under promise and over deliver.

3. Push yourself. Try raising your prices a bit higher than you anticipated or ask for something that you normally would be afraid to ask for, like payment in advance or at least a deposit. I know this might seem trite, but go have lunch by yourself, maybe bring a book, sit at a table not at the bar. After you've accomplished this, do the same thing a movie.

4. Learn something new. Take a course, go back to school, enhance your ability, do something that will give you more credibility, which in turn you'll create an increase in your level of confidence.

5. What's something you really are uncomfortable doing? Do it.

6. Go look at yourself in the mirror. What are you wearing? Did you give this some thought or just grab what was on the top of the pile. Dress for success. Do your hair. Trim your beard. Take care of your body and soul. Looking your best can help you feel your best.

7. Survey your customers. Ask them how you're doing. You might be ⁿrised to learn the truth. While this may take a whack at your ｋing what's broken will get you back on track and inevitably

Pricing Your Practice

increase your confidence.

8. Be nice to everyone. Give as much as you can. Help others. feeling of giving and the kindness you'll receive in return will lift you.

9. Start small and grow. Sell your package at a price you feel comfortable with. Next time, raise it by 10%.

10. Fix the other things in your life that may harm your level of confidence. Marriage, kids, school, cost of living, etc., if any are out of line or acting up, your confidence will be challenged.

11. Bonus: Focus on your diet, get some real exercise, and gosh darn it, have some fun! Take care of your body, feed it right, lose those extra pounds, and enjoy the ride. Failure to do these things will lead to confidence issues, I can practically guarantee it. I've never heard anyone who lost 10 pounds working out say, "I hate the way I look and feel."

P.S. If you need more, start over. Give it time. It will work! Is your mind set?

CHAPTER FIVE
The Psychology of Pricing

The Three Pricing Options

In most marketing books, you'll learn to provide options. If you provide three options, the low and the high help sell the middle. People like to be in the middle.

Sometimes you will learn to put the higher price to the left, sometimes to the right. Not sure which works best, and what colors make us hungry, or the rarified air in Vegas casino or the notes played on slot machines, but what I can tell you is it's all about psychology. The goal is to get you to buy more. I once read that Baskin Robbins uses pink and orange because they learned these colors make us hungry. I'm pretty sure I'm already hungry when I walk into an ice cream shop, but every bit helps right? The point is we are guided by what happens in life. What we experience, who we meet, the results of our favorite team sport, whatever it is, it affects us and moves us, one way or another.

Pricing is partly based on perception and to many, the perception can be altered by providing comparisons, testimonials, videos, or other elements that lead someone to buy your service. The three pricing options is an example of some of the tools used to market and help guide the sales process. The prospective customer will see the balance of the "middle" priced item, if properly designed. The needed services should be included, and only the services rarely in demand are added to the higher priced option. The higher priced option is specialized, and intended as an upgrade. You should almost have your prospective client thinking, "I feel privileged to be someone who selected your highest priced option. It's built for only the top tier firms, like me." The lowest priced option should never be sold. Both from the customer's perspective and your own. You never want to work with bargain hunters who purchase your services at the lowest level and secretly expect more. They do and they will, and you'll end up regretting doing business with them if that's the case.

Higher Pricing Higher Value

Assuming your pricing is within reason, often the low price leader is challenged due to the level of clientele aka "bargain hunters" and questioned by some. Would you seek the lowest priced doctor to do surgery on your child? If a professional doesn't believe in their pricing, how can they believe in themselves? They lack confidence and nothing worse than a surgeon who lacks confidence. Well, the same holds true in any profession. People that know what they are doing are not going to charge the least amount. This is a fact. If they are, beware.

CHAPTER SIX
Selling Your Pricing

The Importance of Selling

Generally, when we think of pricing, we don't consider the importance of being able to sell it. If you are an accounting pro, this is generally not top of mind for you. The fact that you are a business owner however, requires that you learn to sell yourself and your services. Without that ability, you simply cannot operate.

Selling should not be easy. You should have to explain, and you should have to argue why you are a better choice. If it's too easy, your pricing is too low. A reasonable price requires explanation. A high price requires even more, perhaps a good story behind it or some logic or even demonstrate the calculations. If you take the time to calculate your pricing, it legitimatizes it in the mind of your prospective customer. Remember, pricing is a perception, and you need to help create the best perception you can.

Your Pricing Story

Some might call it the reason behind your pricing or the calculations that led you to your pricing structure. Those are handy, but in the end, it's the story. I could very easily price this book at $9.74 rather than the max of $9.99. While I may be losing 25% of $.25 in doing so, it sure would be more attractive to sell my book with a 74 in it. Reminder: My company 74 Systems and it's parent 74 Degrees LLC are named after the ideal temperature of my charming little town of Santa Barbara, where I have lived for over 33 years.

See what I just did there? I made it personal. I made it real. I gave it some flavor and made it mine, unique and more palatable for the buyer. I'm willing to sacrifice profits for the longer term goal of having a better story to sell my book.

If you are an accounting pro, your story can be related to your education. Perhaps you name your pricing after you three favorite bars on High Street in Columbus (assuming you are a big Buckeyes fan like me, this would work). I would offer Mean Mr. Mustards, Papa Joes and of course Tribeca. Means nothing to you, but it's telling my story. I could even apply this same logic to the numbers as I did before. Each pricing option could end in the number of the streets surrounding the university, or maybe my favorite dorm room friends room number, or maybe the flight numbers I took to get to Columbus. There are endless possibilities, but adding a story to anything you need to sell, creates conversation opportunity, and this helps move things along, particularly when you are not the low price leader.

ORNSA

It wouldn't be right to have a chapter on sales without discussing my favorite acronym learned at IBM. ORNSA is a great guide to helping you sell and close customers. Let's break it down...

O = Open Ended Questions - Get the conversation to flow openly. No yes or no questions.

R = Reference - Refer to something that relates to the conversation, like another client you helped in a similar situation.

N = Needs (qualify) - Determine what services they need from you. Check outside for the car they drove to your office in. If it's a Lexus or Tesla, things are probably more in your favor.

S = Solution Sell - Define the service you deliver, explain the price, how to get started and...

A = Action Plan - Close them! Will that be VISA or MC? Tuesday or Thursday work? Here, giving them a closed ended question works, but only if there are limited responses. Do not offer a "n/a" option or a "let me think about it."

Let me also put it into a narrative for you that you can translate and repurpose. Ready?

Tell me more about your business and why you chose to become an accounting professional? Oh, so you got your accounting degree at Ohio State? No way. My brother played quarterback there. I'm from Cleveland. I'm a huge Buckeye fan. So you need more clients and you are prepared to commit the time and pay my fees to get it done. I think we should start with your pricing structure. How's Tuesday at 3pm or I can even do today at 4pm, which works best? Great. Click this link and let's

Eric Greenspan

get started.

CHAPTER SEVEN
Pricing Perception

Pricing Is Sold On Perception

Pricing is often sold on perception. We look at a provider, consider their services, examine their pricing, listen to their pitch, read their testimonials, and then we decide whether or not to hire them. We perceive them to something and their pricing is a reflection of them. If we hire them, we are under the perception that they can deliver and that they are charging an acceptable price. We really don't know until they start doing the job and our perception is likely to change after learning what and how they deliver their services. This pricing perception is a psychological component of the sales process. The more we perceive their value to be, the higher the price we're willing to pay. Conversely, if they charge less than what we perceive to be "within the range" we might question whether they can sustain operations or we identify that they lack confidence. Neither are good, and neither would lead me to choose this provider.

We often hire people because we just feel good about them. We're not always right. But there was something we perceived about this person, the way they spoke, their own belief in themselves, maybe how they looked at us in our eyes and acknowledge their own weakness. Whatever it was, it had a lot to do with their confidence and our perception was that they would do a good job for us.

Sometimes, it's just a great sales job. The provider turned out to be ordinary, but they got me to buy. That's ok too, from the service provider's perspective. You might not fire them, but you hired them based on a different perception than reality. I think part of this is we as people want to think highly of others, particularly when they are offering to assist us in some way.

The balance of pricing perception is also important as it provides insight into

Pricing Your Practice

the difference of how we perceive our own value versus what our customers perceive. When that balance is out of alignment, we are at risk and you should work towards evening the balance. Simply put, if our customer's perception of our value is less than our own perception, we may have trouble getting paid, and we are at risk of losing the customer. If the balance is flipped, we need to raise our prices.

Your Perception

If the pricing perception balance is in your favor, meaning you are perceived as a great value, you might be leaving money on the table. When we price ourselves too low and our customers know it, they're unlikely to send us extra money, even though they'd gladly pay more. The longer this goes on, the harder it will be to change it. We become a part of their budget, and they deem us a fixed cost, which means they won't want it to change. But that's our fault for allowing it in the first place. We should never be considered a fixed cost. Our services are valuable and we are only going to get better.

We should always establish price changes in our engagement letters, alerting our clients that we may raise our prices from time to time. We should also make sure to test the Pricing perception balance regularly to ensure it remains in balance.

Your Clients' Perception

If the pricing perception balance is high on from your perspective and low from your client's, you may risk losing the client. While it's easy to raise your prices to balance perception, it's often hard to prove your value after the fact, as the initial perception is sticky. In this case, we often find ourselves adding something to make up for the shortcoming, and this can lead to stress and lack of focus on the customers where balance is properly level.

Lowering your price will create other issues. My biggest concern here is animosity towards this client. They cannot be your favorite, if you have to accommodate a price reduction on their behalf. You might just work a little harder for your better paying clients, and that can only end badly.

You can try to resell them on the concept as to why your price is what it is. The longer you keep them around, the more in balance you will become according to the laws of economics or at least from my experience. What I mean is eventually you'll catch up, as costs rise and pricing increases are expected over time.

Either way, it's not a good place to be so be careful to always make sure your clients perceive your services equal to your own perception. You will have fewer issues, less turnover, and happier clients and staff.

CHAPTER EIGHT
Pricing Models

Hourly

When I got divorced last, my attorney asked me for a $7,500 retainer. He sent me an old school engagement letter in the mail. In it, somewhere buried in the middle of 12 pages were instructions on sending the retainer. I honestly never saw it.

He called one day and was angry. He wanted his payment. I asked and explained. He didn't care and told me to send the money. Truth be told, I figured I'd get a bill in the mail or even an email. Someone needs to re-evaluate the pricing and sales process of this firm. Oh, and when I asked him where we were in relation to the retainer, he told me, "we spent that long ago…in fact you have a rather large balance and we need payment now." How did I not know this? How did he spent that many hours and we had accomplished NOTHING to date? My value perception of him was very low. I fired him.

Let's start with what hourly pricing claims to solve (from the provider perspective) and the first of the problems (the same issue but from the client perspective). Hourly billing helps the service provider account for their time. So you are selling time. I get it. But how does that provide the customer any comfort? What do I get for that time? How long will it take? When does it end? Shouldn't delivery of services be the intent? Hourly billing opens the flood gates for endless billing with no assurance for results. It puts customers into a panic, as it did me above. There simply is no accountability and it's just too easy to "pad the bill." It also turns this industry into a commodity, something that has already hurt pricing levels.

Hourly pricing, when used properly can be effective. Sadly, it's not often used properly and for bookkeepers and tax professionals, what might take you very little time, yet has tremendous value, might not be in your best interest to charge hourly. Let's say you setup automation to do the matching on the bank feeds. When they download, the code you helped write or the app you pay for is doing the job well. But you still have responsibility here. It might only take you 5 minutes to check to see if its working, but that 5 minutes and that app are worth 1% of your client's revenue. You know why? Because having your books in order is not only a critical and required function for a successful company, it's also a gift to the business owner to be able to plan, and identify trends, secure financing, and grow. You are providing a valuable service, when you do your job right. I don't care if you it took you 3 hours once to setup, and 5 minutes a day to manage. Set a price that equals its value and maintain that price as your client's revenue soars.

Value Pricing

Value pricing provides an alternative to hourly. As a provider, we can and should track our time, but our goal now is to spend as little time as possible, not as much. If we can do in a minute, what was once billed as an hour, the value would then be determined by what we produce, not by some kind of unit, such as time or FTE. We would be valued by our work product, and our results. In this case, everyone wins.

Imagine if a fast food chain paid it's employees for how many burgers they sold or made, or how many times they cleaned the tables, or swept the floor, rather than by the hour. More burgers would be sold, faster. Floors and tables would be cleaner. If they make the burger wrong, they get a deduction. If so, they'd rarely get a burger wrong and I'd bet they'd check it twice before stuffing it in the bag. Customer service would rise, ensuring more repeat business, and the best employees would get more and be cherished. They would be paid for their value, not their time. The business would pay based on success, not mediocrity or failure. Imagine that?

A risk of value pricing is providers often fail to maintain the levels. The "set it and forget it" happens often and does not account for increases in costs or overhead. Therefore, it is very important to maintain your value pricing levels. Over time, you need to increase the pricing and you should build this into your engagement letters, so it's not a surprise to your client when it happens. Even so, they may act surprised, but at least you have it in black and white, which will help maintain their value perception of your and your firm. While this is a negative to value pricing, it is easy to manage. Keep tight controls on it and evaluate it annually, build into your engagement letters, and you should be fine.

Eric Greenspan

If you are in the accounting or bookkeeping industry, you likely already know about value pricing and you probably know or at least have heard of Ron Baker. I'm not skilled enough to speak on his behalf, but I can tell you one thing about Ron and value pricing…it just makes sense. To learn more about value pricing, I recommend you read Ron's book "Implementing Value Pricing: A Radical Business Model for Professional Firms."

Project Based Pricing

Sometimes we just need to deliver something and we can negotiate a set price, take a retainer or deposit, and do it, get paid, and move on. The risks associated with Project Based Pricing often relate to perception of the deliverable. You can ensure success with a proper scope document or statement of work, but this is usually requested prior to the engagement being accepted, so it's on your time, your dollar, and your risk. For that very reason, I generally avoid this billing method or ask for a non refundable fee for the scope document creation as security. I allow them to continue or keep the document to hire someone else should they wish to do so. I charge a premium for this as the risk is high.

Another way you can used Project Based Pricing is as a starter but do so with a limit on the period or a sliding scale.

In the case of a limit, you'd be offering a fixed price for the first month. After the month, you'd then evaluate and explain or "sell" your position to the client. You can tell them what you achieved and then have an open discussion as to what value that provides them. If they argue the price was too high, perhaps now with a little experience, you can offer a slimmed down version of the service at a lower price, but now, the expectations are completely in alignment. I like to do projects this way, if I see potential for an ongoing relationship.

In the case of the sliding scale, you set thresholds for the base and depending on the result, can scale up, not down. I personally see this as always appearing as a negative, should you slide that scale up. People expect too much sometimes, and they will question your integrity or whether you know your business well enough. I would avoid this if possible.

You may also add some criteria that would be added in addition should certain things occur. If they do, send an additional invoice. It's a bit like that divorce attorney of mine, with the over billing and nitpicking of copies, stamps, and whatever else they could pad the bill with. If it feels wrong, just don't do it.

Percentage Pricing

Ah, my favorite pricing model of all, Percentage Pricing. I'm not saying I invented Percentage Pricing, but I did just start using it one day and then created a Percentage Pricing Calculator to help my clients establish their pricing structure. It was clear that there was a similarity across all of my clients, in particular the percentage their cost represented when compared against the client's revenue.

PP does two things. First, it helps compare your pricing in each of the three pricing structures, PP, value and hourly. Next, it makes it easier for our clients to explain their pricing to their clients. It adds a "story" with structure, rather than an arbitrary number created based on what they "think" might be appropriate. We now have a reason, a calculation, and when explained to a prospective client, it helps the prospective client grasp and come to terms with the proposal, so they will sign the engagement letter and hire you.

Percentage pricing uses a tool we created call the Percentage Pricing Calculator. The spreadsheet allows us to create scenarios and enter our client's revenue, a percentage (usually 1-3%) and determine a value. We then complete the value pricing section, breaking down our price by service. We then "massage" the numbers up and down on each line item until the total matches the PP calculation above. Finally, we enter our current hourly rate, expected number of hours to complete the project each period, and actual hours it took to complete a similar project. We can then raise and lower the hourly rate until the value equals the two above. When this happens, we are in alignment.

But alignment is not always a good thing. At this point, we can determine if the hourly rate we just set when compared to the number of hours is even worth our time to get up each morning. The idea here is to determine if you are earning enough to justify your hard work. You can "feel" if the rate is too high, or too low, but more importantly, you will be able to determine the number of hours you are committing to the process. You will start to identify that your hourly rate needs to be modified and the number of hours to complete the project must follow. You have to find a comfortable spot here, somewhere between "I'm worth that price for an hour of hard work" and "I'm willing to put that many hours in if my end result is X." This will help you set your value pricing number. This may change your percentage from 1% to 2% and if it does, my work is done here and congratulations.

Lastly, by continually evaluating pricing over the years, you can re-use the Percentage Pricing Calculator to make sure your pricing remains in alignment. One of the risks of value pricing is complacency and it worries me, so the importance cannot be over stressed. Often, we ignore our pricing, become complacent, and we may (or perhaps forget) to increase it over time, as we would an hourly rate. Remember, costs will likely rise. If you have to pay more, so do your clients. Use the PPC every six months and never let this happen.

CHAPTER NINE
Setting Your Pricing

Create a Pricing Scale

Start your pricing process by researching your industry and competition. A simple Google search should give you the answers you need. If you are a Tax Preparer, find a few others that have their pricing displayed on their website and build a comparison spreadsheet to get an idea of the average. Look for companies in the same areas you serve, as demographics may need to be factored in.

Next, set a low threshold number for the low side. This number is the number that is the absolute lowest you'd be willing to accept in a payment for a service, both from your gut and from your cost of living. Now set the highest threshold number you think you can sell. You now know your Pricing Scale and somewhere between the low and the high is the number for you. The goal here is to get as close the high as possible and later, reset the thresholds as your knowledge, skills and confidence increase.

As an example, suppose a local tax pro that does very well, has nice digs, drives a fancy car, and is known to be "higher priced" charges $3,000 for a business return that includes a personal filing for a couple as well. For sake of this discussion, let's not worry about structure or which forms they use. Let's assume it's a small business with a husband and wife as owners. If you already in business, let's assume you currently charge roughly half that price for the same service. So that is your low threshold. Your high threshold would be as close to that $3,000 as you can get. I say go for it.

For startups, same idea as above but you have no lower threshold. You can do one of two things. First, you can find a lower priced provider and set your lower threshold based on their pricing and the high as close to the higher priced provider as mentioned above. The second options is to simply test the

Pricing Your Practice

waters by asking for a number somewhere in the Pricing Scale you set and trying to close some business. If this fails, and you are either losing business or finding yourself discounting to close them, you can either work on your confidence or simply lower the pricing for the next opportunity. I would start 10-20% above the lower threshold and build from there. Each time, add a little more. As your business and confidence grows, so will your price for services.

When I was at IBM, I asked my boss if I could come with him on a big pitch to UCSB. He didn't let me go; he said I wasn't ready. He was right. He told me to sell one computer. I did. Then he told me to sell 3. Then 30. And so on. Start small, grow, build and reach for the stars. Oh, by the way, the deal he went on he lost. He was selling IBM RISC workstations to the UCSB computer lab. His competition was NEXT and they won the gig. Steve Jobs, after being rehired by Apple, later brought NEXT into create the new Mac OS. I wish I was at that sale now!

Your Current Pricing

This process is actually quite easy. Are you happy?

If you answered yes, then ask yourself, "Would more income make you even happier?"

If you answered no, you can stop reading or just read for enjoyment. But if you answered no to the first question and yes to the second or at least yes to the second question, let's do this.

First thing to do is compare your pricing to your competition. Have a friend call and ask for a quote. Search the web for their pricing pages. See if they others are discussing it in Google or Yelp reviews. Once you find out a few others pricing levels, you can then compare to your own. If they are all equal and you are not having trouble closing new customers, then your entire industry is below the pricing threshold and do NOT let this stop you from raising your prices.

Let's assume you find out that you are 35% below two of your competitors. You should seriously consider raising your prices. You don't have to do it all at once and you can do it without risking loss of clients. You may lose a couple, but those are the ones you probably want to get rid of anyhow. Generally, the toughest clients are also the ones that pay the least. A great client wants to pay you, needs you, and values you.

Now, let's go with the scenario that your priced at the top of the market, having no trouble with closing new business, and still want to raise your prices. First, you should. Then, see the next chapter.

Planning Your Pricing

If you're just getting started, now is the time to plan your pricing for future growth and building in the process of price increases. As costs of living increase, and at least in my experience, they always have, it's important to stay in line with pricing increases, to keep your margins and profits in sync. Evaluate your pricing annually to ensure you are keeping up with current cost of living increases, should they exist, your competition, and alignment with your always growing skillset. Have you added new services and have you added them into the pricing structure?

Rarely in life does the price of a service decline, except perhaps during corrections, so give some thought about what you would do if the economy tanked and people still needed your help. Rather than lowering pricing, consider a temporary "disaster recovery" or "economy recovery plan" to help keep business flowing.

When planning pricing, remember that only you know what you can do and what you cannot do. But more importantly, remember that you can always learn and grow. What I mean is don't let your lack of skills or ability hold you back. Conversely, don't overprice yourself if you are unable to deliver. Clearly in the beginning you may have to price yourself a bit lower, but be sure to remind your clients that you are giving them a lower price now, and it won't remain this way forever. Set the expectation of a price increase early, and make sure you work hard, grow and earn the right to raise your prices.

Open your calendar and put in dates to evaluate your pricing every six months or at least annually. Add this list in the notes:

1. Evaluate current pricing vs. current expenses and overhead.

2. Evaluate current pricing vs. current skill set.

3. Evaluate current pricing vs. competitors (try to use the same competitors used initially and monitor their changes in skills, services provided and price.)

4. Evaluate level of confidence and determine if you feel more confident, stronger and willing to earn more, maintaining the same level of sales closing ratio if the price was higher. Test it.

5. Evaluate current services offered. Are you getting paid what you deserve?

Profitability

How important are profits? To be blunt, they are the only thing that ultimately matters. You are not working to pay overhead. You are working to pay for greens fees, fillings, meals, and college tuition. If your pricing merely covers your overhead and leaves no room for the good things in life, such as those mentioned above, others like them, plus your salary, then there's no need to analyze the industry to determine your pricing just yet. What you really need to do first is structure your pricing so you cover your overhead, put a little aside, and pay yourself really well. The better you pay yourself, the healthier your company. Profits are key to success, and should be recognized early on in your pricing. If this is not the case, ignore everything I said above and figure this part out first. If you can't find a profit in your pricing after raising them to the high threshold, you need to go back and examine your costs and overhead. Something just isn't right and now is the time to fix it.

Another note on profit, a pal of mine Mike Michalowicz wrote one of the most popular books in our industry called Profit First. I always wanted to be an author after my first call with this guy. Anyhow, Mike and I have shared the stage and mic and webcam from time to time. He looks great in a vest. I'm a cap kind of guy. But in all seriousness, considering Profit First is timely when creating or changing our pricing. The profit that you will shave off the top and transfer to another account, should be built right in to your pricing from the beginning. Regardless if you adopt Mike's idea here, you should always know what is overhead and what is profit, in every dollar you earn.

Opportunity Cost

Of course costs matter, but this is not a book about costs. It's a book about price. But we must take opportunity cost into consideration when we establish our pricing. Opportunity cost is simply the cost of missed opportunities that occur due to poor pricing practices or wasting time on non income producing activities. We need to be careful that improper pricing can lead to lost opportunities as there are only so many hours in a day, so use them wisely and ensure you are getting paid what you are worth.

Naming Your Pricing

Basic, pro, expert? Silver, gold, platinum? I mean if that's what makes you happy, do it. But you can do better. Start by examining yourself, where you live, how you are different and then try again. E.g. if you live in Texas, on a ranch, you could name your packages Pony, Quarter Horse, Thoroughbred. Like to fish? How about Guppie, Small Mouth, Large Mouth or Perch, Salmon, Tuna, Shark, Whale.

You don't have to this, but when you make your business about you, it's easier to sell and easier for others to grasp your pitch. My company is called 74 Systems, a DBA of 74 Degrees LLC. Santa Barbara, where we live and work, has an average temperature of 74 degrees. It's also the perfect temperature in my opinion. My mom would call her company 120 Degrees, if following suit, as she lives in Palm Desert, California.

I am going to change the name of pricing for the Ignite Program right now. I love planes. Lets see what I come up with.

CHAPTER TEN
Adjusting Your Pricing

How to Adjust Pricing Now

Adjusting your pricing is something you do internally. You must decide the level of the increase. Do NOT ask your customers for their input. It's simply not their business. You run your company. What you deliver to them is all that matters. Your costs and pricing strategy is for you to decide and remember you must believe in it, or you will not be able to sell it.

That said, remember about pricing perception balance. You DO want to ensure your clients perceive your current and future pricing properly and to maintain the balance as we discussed previously.

Generally, we tell our clients to raise pricing in 10-20% increments annually until they reach their upper threshold goal. So if you are the company that charges one half of the $3,000 for a tax return, or $1,500, from this day forward your pricing should be $1,500 * 1.20 = $1,800 for new clients. I'd also raise existing clients 10% to $1,650.

New clients are easy. You just send the engagement letters. If you have pricing on your website, adjust it accordingly.

For existing clients, send the engagement letters as you normally would. If you have only been in business a short time, 5 years or less, just send them with the new pricing. If you are 5+ years in business, consider including a small blurb in the letter about the price increase. Do not over explain it. Say something like, "From time to time, we must adjust our pricing. Thank you for your patronage." No reason to explain why. They know why. And no reason to call too much attention to it. If they call and complain, and you do NOT wish to lose that particular customer, tell them you will grandfather them based on prior pricing for this year but next year they will be subject to the increase. Just say, send it, move on. If they leave, find a better client. I can practically guarantee you that the biggest complainers will be the clients you wouldn't mind never working with again.

Maintain Your Pricing Levels

Each year, repeat this procedure until you have reached your threshold. After you have reached your threshold, recheck your "higher priced" competitors and stay in line with them or if you feel the market will bear it and you can sell it, become the highest priced in the industry. Do this with caution however. If you are the highest priced, you also must be the best. Continue adding to your skills and delivering the best you can deliver.

Another concern for being the highest priced is a shift in the economy. Should this happen, you will most likely have to lower your prices. Or, if you are really that good, you will be able to maintain. Everyone gets hurt in a downturn in the economy, but the best survive. Ironically, your services might become even more in demand in a bad economy. Your competition, at least the ones that are not enrolled at schoolofbookkeeping.com or schooloftaxes.com or the Ignite Program, or have not read this book, will suffer more than you. That is to your advantage and you should feel pretty good about it. How's that for a confidence booster?

Remember this list? Be sure you followed this step and add to your calendar, putting in dates to evaluate your pricing every six months or at least annually. Add this list in the notes:

1. Evaluate current pricing vs. current expenses and overhead.

2. Evaluate current pricing vs. current skill set.

3. Evaluate current pricing vs. competitors (try to use the same competitors used initially and monitor their changes in skills, services provided and price.)

4. Evaluate level of confidence and determine if you feel more confident, stronger and willing to earn more, maintaining the same level of sales closing ratio if the price was higher. Test it.

5. Evaluate current services offered. Are you getting paid what you deserve?

Tom, CPA

Tom is a great client. I have always enjoyed our meetings. Much of the work we did initially was to automate processes, eliminate the barrage of phone and email messages, and build a system for managing workflow. Today, Tom is rarely interrupted and his work gets done faster and without distraction. Tom is happier, more productive and making more money.

Beyond that, Tom is the perfect client to talk about here in regards to pricing. Tom has been in business for many years, and he's not raised his prices in a long time. So we did. Tom was worried that he would hear back from many of them complaining about the increase. Ironically, the only few he actually heard from were clients he'd rather be rid of anyhow. One of them complained about the rate increase and hasn't paid for last years taxes. Sound familiar?

I worked closely with Tom on how to handle objections. He handled them perfectly. He stood firm, as right he should. The guy is giving his customers a deal, and they know it. In the end, very few put up a fuss. They just the paid the new pricing and when on with their lives.

As Tom and I worked together, Tom began expanding his extracurricular activities. Tom is a kickboxing instructor. He used to walk in to his classes unprepared and a bit stressed. But as he learned and his confidence grew, Tom now owns the process. Other instructors give him the stink eye because he doesn't need to create a syllabus. He just walks in and gets it done.

Tom also runs marathons. No need to give the details here, but know that Tom is doing this for his health, his love for athletics and fitness, and the benefits he's achieved are plenty, much of it attributed to strengthening his confidence.

Ongoing, all new clients at Tom's firm are set at the new pricing levels. Tom is making more money than ever, and working smarter. He got through the last season with less stress than the many years prior, and more money in the bank to carry him through to the next season. Now, we are focusing on that next season and Tom is going to love what comes next. We will be automating the entire on boarding process, from engagement letters, to organizers, to document collections, and more. The systems we used last season are in place, the staff is trained to use them, so we will hit the ground running.

CHAPTER ELEVEN
Billing Systems, Payments, Credit

Overview

Getting paid is a challenge many face. I'm not specifically referring to the act of collections, but just finding the right tools to invoice or track or automate billing and payments. QuickBooks and Xero and other other accounting software can handle this for us, but require manual creation of invoices or recurring billing. Learning about and establishing a relationship with payment providers can guide what products and methods we might choose. We also need a little help or some skill to build this into our website or configure a cloud app to manage the process.

I'm going to focus on my favorite process for getting paid which is directly on my Wordpress website with a few add-ons and some newer, sophisticated and tech savvy payments systems.

For example, if you look towards the new payment systems such as Stripe, Square and PayPal, you will see a big difference from the traditional payment systems provided by a bank, a third party or in conjunction with something like Authorize.net. We will break each down in this chapter so you can get a better understanding of how each are used and why. Each of these systems make the process of implementing, tracking and even automating the billing process.

We will also discuss the credit offers from some of these processors, as they built in and you should know about them. They don't directly relate to pricing, but I would be doing you a disservice not sharing what I know about them each.

Subscriptions

I love subscriptions. I hate invoicing and net terms. Even when it says due and payable, people pay over time. My last company, which grew substantially for 11 years and then in year 12 due to the remnants of the Great Recession and a bad choice in direction, failed. Along the way however, we built systems that allowed us to get paid immediately after the job. As a tech services company, we went door to door solving mostly residential technology problems. After each appointment, we held out our Blackberries and a cellular payment device and took a credit card. We often sold a prepaid support agreement at the same time. They were NOT subscriptions. I truly wish they were. But we always got paid and the money would be in the bank faster, and with less accounting work.

As we built that company I remember a customer once saying, "You can't charge for your services on the job. You'll never achieve success that way. You need to invoice us so we have time to write a check and mail it." I responded to him, "Do you do this at the grocery store? How about after a manicure or when your cleaning person leaves?" He said that's different. I said that's ok. We failed in year 12, but I can absolutely guarantee you our payment policy had no bearing on the failure. We had over 44,000 client testimonials and NO ONE ever complained about the payment process. We changed the way they did things, a little, and today, getting paid in advance for services or immediately after is becoming the status quo. Even my plumber and electrician do it.

I had an uncle once in past life. He ran a company called Scotty's Piper Plumbing. He wasn't Scottish, his name wasn't Scotty, and he did not play the bagpipes. At the end of each appointment, serving an affluent Florida suburb, he'd turn to the client and say, "All done. Time to pay the piper." It worked every time.

There are many ways to build a subscription system, but my favorite is with Woocommerce on a Wordpress website. It's easy to setup, easy to manage, and extremely reliable. The best part is Woocommerce has extensions for just about any payments processor. This means you can create your products or subscriptions on your website, enable and integrate your payment processor, and be up and running in minutes.

Woocommerce is free and some payment processor plugins are free too, such as Stripe, Square and PayPal. You can even enable Amazon payments which is really cool since it has all the credit cards you've setup in your Amazon account readily available. This makes the buying process that much easier for your customers. You can hide the product pages or expose them publicly, your choice.

Subscriptions on Woocommerce require an additional extension and while you have to pay for it, it's very reasonably priced. The purchase and subscription are managed automatically by Woocommerce, which triggers renewals and payments, and handles communications with you and your customers.

Stripe

Stripe is very technically savvy and slick. It has a great interface and a strong API. It's really easy to setup and configure and has a great iPhone app. Like PayPal, Stripe refunds the fee if you refund the purchase and only charges per transaction. There is no monthly fee.

Do be aware that Stripe is not your advocate for dispute resolution. If someone files a claim, you are likely to lose. You can share your terms (mine say absolutely no refunds in 18pt type) and most often, Stripe gives in to the bank.

Conversely, if you have failed payments, Stripe will work hard to retry them (so will Woocommerce) automatically. They "recover" failed transactions well.

I have not learned of Stripe offering credit facilities, but have heard a few rumors. The idea of why they would is the credit offer is tied to your volume and retains their customers. The more volume you process, the higher the credit line, so you just stick with them to get the highest credit line possible. While not offered yet by Stripe, PayPal has mastered that and we'll discuss it in later in this chapter.

QuickBooks Payments

QuickBooks Payments is an old school system. It was once owned by a bank, later acquired by Intuit. It works great though, and it's relatively easy to use and configure. It lacks an app for mobile and it has a flaw in its design. Conversely, it has something no one else can match and it's a home run in my honest opinion.

The flaw is their refund policy. When a transaction is refunded, meaning you refund your customer, other providers refund the discount fee (~2.9%) for the original transaction. Stripe and PayPal refund the discount fee and do NOT charge any other transaction fees either direction. QuickBooks Payments is unique in that it charges a transaction fee and a discount fee in both directions, if after the batch has processed. If you have a lot of refunds, I would avoid it. If not, it's the best choice by far. It also has ACH options and they are really inexpensive.

Now, putting the aforementioned flaw aside, it is a pittance in comparison the benefit you receive using QB Payments as this product automatically matches your bank deposits with invoices. This reduces your workload tremendously and almost always makes it worthwhile as the product of choice.

Also, if you are a bookkeeper or accounting professional and you either use or sell QuickBooks, QuickBooks Payments, or Payroll, join the Complete Business Partner program from Carrie Kahn and save a bundle on fees and share in commissions. Learn more at completebusinesspartner.com.

Square

Square, like Stripe, is also very technically savvy and slick. It has a great interface too, but it was initially designed for point of sale and mainly it's own. It's great for a small retail shop, but it lacks subscriptions native to Woocommerce and for that reason, I don't use it.

PayPal

PayPal is pretty amazing. They have so many different services all tied together. You can use traditional PayPal for payments, credit cards, and you setup "Apply for PayPal Credit" and then offer it on your website as a payment type. You can get Working Capital loans in an instant if you are doing volume, credit cards, and now they offer Loan Builder (acquired from Swift) as an alternative loan product with fast turn around times and impressive limits and rates.

If you do in fact use PayPal with Woocommerce, I highly recommend using the version known as Braintree PayPal. The difference is they have a plugin that keeps your customers on your site, rather than being redirected to PayPal to make the purchase. It's free and just works better. It will also setup credit cards alongside the PayPal option. Braintree made a better PayPal interface and PayPal now owns Braintree as a result.

Unlike Stripe, the dispute process on PayPal is better and more in your favor. If you can provide that someone paid for your service, and you did everything right, including clear terms and a process for them to accept them, you have a better chance of winning.

Another great feature of PayPal is instant transfer. Need cash flow? Pay 1% and PayPal will put the money in your bank account within seconds. Sometimes this is worth. For me, I think it's always worth it.

Expanding on the credit offers PayPal provides, Working Capital is pretty slick. They approved based on volume over time. They'll give you about 30% of your transaction volume and they do it in an instant. Then, depending on the option you select, they take small payments, 1-30% I think, of each payment transaction you receive. If you don't get a payment, you don't pay. They just shave off their part and leave the rest for you to transfer to your bank.

Loan Builder works differently. You get a loan, fast, but you pay it back in weekly payments auto debited from your account and it matters not if you have cash in that account. They'll take it out one way or another. Risky if cash flow is tight. But I did it and 12 months later the payments stopped. It was like losing 20 pounds and felt great and the capital helped us expand. When used properly, these alternative funding options can be great as you establish your business and get your pricing up high enough to no longer need capital.

Amazon Payments

Amazon Payments is a cool add on for Woocommerce as it literally lets you connect your Amazon profile and specifically the payment accounts so that whatever you store in Amazon as a payment method can easily be applied at checkout on your site. There's no catch here and it's a free plugin. The rule of thought in this industry is give as many payment options as possible. While people many get overwhelmed by too many pricing options, payment options are systematically tried until one goes through, or chosen as a favorite. I almost always choose PayPal credit. I get to pay over time and I can max out the line and they don't report to the credit bureaus!

Pay Over Time

We already discussed PayPal credit and how you can literally put a button on your checkout page so your customers can apply and use PayPal credit. But they are not alone in the space. Affirm and Klarna are two companies that offer such services for online commerce systems and they work a little differently.

Affirm is my favorite. I was in a Peloton store with my family about 6 months ago. We really wanted the Peloton bike but it was over $2,0000 and we had just moved our home. When the sales rep explained we could do interest free payments over time through Affirm, we bought the bike. We pay $52/mo for the Peloton and since it's interest free, it's interest earning as the money we would have spent is in the bank earning us interest, rather than earning someone else interest. Affirm is found on many of the leading websites today as a payment option. I bought my Nest Protects (smoke and carbon monoxide detectors with wifi) interest free.

Beyond the checkout with Affirm, they also have a "pre-approval" model where you can apply with no harm to your credit score and they may or may not give you an amount that you can have sent to you on a credit card to your inbox immediately. You may then use this card anywhere! The payment terms are fair and the interest rates are fabulous.

Lastly about Affirm, they have a great app and a great website. Easy to use would be an understatement. But my favorite feature is they allow you to turn on or off auto pay and they charge the same either way. Also, if you pay off early, the interest is eliminated. It's not front loaded either, so you save on all remaining interest if it exists and paid early.

Eric Greenspan

Klarna is similar in many ways, but I've not found it as frequent or as simple to use. I did want to mention it and I apologize for my lack of knowledge on this tool. I do know you can easily apply to become a Klarna partner. I did, but it's been months and they've not responded. I may try again soon.

CHAPTER TWELVE
What Else Can You Do To Earn More?

Automate Everything

We have talked in detail about pricing, but there are other ways to increase your profits. The obvious is costs reduction. But the better one is automation. The cost to automate an app or process in today's world is likely significantly less than the time it takes to manually perform the same task. If that's true, then automate it.

I'm a huge fan of insightly and Zapier. The two work well together, but then again, Zapier works well with so many apps. Zapier is simply an automation tool that takes something from one app or when that app "triggers" something and then adds it or changes something in another app. E.g. When a new lead is added in insightly, add that lead to a MailChimp list and email the lead using Gmail using a template you define. Inside of insightly is Workflow Automation, a tool that creates the triggers you can use in Zapier. E.g. Trigger to this URL when the new lead is added so Zapier can retrieve it and do what you tell it to do next.

New on the scene is Siri Shortcuts. So far, I've built a few automations here. App support is somewhat limited, but it is brand new and ironically, Zapier already has instructions on how to use the two together. Automation is happening and you should take advantage.

Mailchimp can be setup to automatically send a series of emails, abandoned shopping cart reminders, and other triggered by events.

CoSchedule can automate and regurgitate your social media content. It integrates beautifully with Wordpress and allows you to share a post in seconds that will requeue and send again in say a month or maybe two. It's a great way to share your content and automate it as you grow it.

Pricing Your Practice

Even QuickBooks can be automated. I am paid using Woocommerce Subscriptions. Each payment is automatically added to QuickBooks Online from a Zap and each has two line items. The first for the sale and the second to deduct the fee. Boom!

Finally, one of my favorite tools for handling support or customer emails is GrooveHQ. It's both a ticketing system for group support and a knowledge base all integrated so offer self service. This tool makes managing incoming emails easier by sharing the ones that are shareable to other team members. Some of the emails never get sent now, as the knowledge base gives them a way to get answers faster, and without your intervention. E.g. If your clients are always calling for the same thing, teach them to use the knowledge base and put the article explaining the answer in it. When they start typing the email it will find the article and they will get their answer and not need to send you the email they started.

Offer Higher Valued Services

We can increase our revenue and profits by adding services that are high in demand, but under served. These types of services require additional education. I'm pretty sure those of you with the highest CS# will take this to heart.

A great example for tax pros is to offer tax resolution services. Helping people that are in a jam is highly specialized, and if you get good at it, you can excel and grow your practice fast.

If you're a bookkeeper, establish strong bonds with tax pros or add specialized services such as sales tax management, or payroll. I think the best area of opportunity in the bookkeeping industry is e-commerce and point of sale, but only because I know there are not many focused on this and many need your help.

Never Stop Learning

You should always keep the learning machine in motion. Never become complacent. You are a business owner, an entrepreneur, and the day you stop being that, is the day of your demise. You might not fail as a result, but you definitely will stop achieving at the same rate you once did. Save that for your retirement. Don't let it be forced upon you because you weren't excited anymore and stopped paying attention to the little things.

About

I'm Eric Greenspan and I'm a father of two boys and stepfather to others, living on the bleeding edge of technology and innovation. My passion is fierce in everything I do. Whether it's parenting, building a company, travel, sports or whipping up the perfect Caesar salad, I commit to excellence, always. I'm a ferocious entrepreneur that has a love for marketing, technology, automation, organization and making things work. I love creating mind blowing customer experiences and developing systems that get it done with as few clicks as possible. My companies operate under 74 Degrees LLC, where I am Chief Clever Officer at 74 Systems, and Chief Education Officer at schoolofbookkeeping.com. I absolutely love what I do.

At 74 Systems, I help accounting pros Ignite their practice with marketing, technology and automation consulting services to assist with client acquisition, sales training, pricing models, workflow management, web and social media and more. Our clients grow fast, adding confidence, clients, skills, revenue and profits.

At schoolofbookkeeping.com, I manage all aspects of the business and handle the company's sales and marketing efforts, business development and technology. I also host our weekly Webinars and write for our blog Too Legit To Audit.

I spend a lot of my time at the keyboard and in the kitchen. I have over 10,000 hours at both. In my early years, I could be found on the municipal golf course in Palm Springs, California picking from plentiful lemon trees and selling lemonade on the second hole. Little did I know that this would be the start of my entrepreneurial career. I have spent my entire adult lifetime building companies. My greatest skill is identifying unique marketing

Pricing Your Practice

opportunities and driving customer acquisition. My last company accumulated over 50,000 customers and most importantly, over 44,000 unique customer testimonials.

Current projects: 74 Systems, schoolofbookkeeping.com, schooloftaxes.com, book writing

CV HIGHLIGHTS:

- Mud Angels, Inc. – Chairman
- insightly "Hero"
- Certified QuickBooks ProAdvisor
- Yelp Elite Squad member 2017 and 2018
- TED attendee 2010-2012
- Licensee and co-producer TEDxAmericanRiviera 2010/2011/2012/2013 (hiatus)
- Sage Summit Speaker
- Accountex Speaker
- Teddy Bear Cancer Foundation: Former Board Member
- Emcee/auctioneer for Saks and the City benefitting Teddy Bear Cancer Foundation
- Emcee for Bears and Bees event benefitting Teddy Bear Cancer Foundation
- Southern California Technology Council: Former Board Member
- Santa Barbara Chamber of Commerce, Former Business Leaders Council
- All Saints by the School fundraising committee (former)
- Montecito Union School: Special fundraising committee, technology advisor, emcee and auctioneer for signature fundraising event for 7 years (former)

Eric Greenspan

- Laguna Blanca prep school technology advisory committee (former)
- Recipient of the Honorary Service Award by the California PTA
- Citrix iBusiness Board of Governors (former)
- Emcee at Convergence (Microsoft campus in Santa Clara) 2010 and 2011
- Recipient of Best Places to Work award from Pacific Coast Business Times
- Two time winner of Best Of in the Santa Barbara Independent for computer repair
- Capstone speaker for USC's CTM event in San Jose at Sun headquarters
- University of Southern California, Marshall School of Business (USC): For 10 years I was a speaker on business building, marketing and PR
- University of California, Los Angeles, Andersen School of Business (UCLA): For 10 years I was a speaker on Entrepreneuring and Extreme Customer Service
- University of California, Santa Barbara (UCSB): Regular speaker, various topics
- Santa Barbara City College: Regular speaker, various topics
- SBCC Scheinfeld Center profiled speaker
- Dos Pueblos Entrepreneuring course guest speaker
- Anacapa prep school guest speaker
- 3 time finalist Entrepreneur of the Year Ernst & Young
- 2 time finalist Entrepreneur of the Year PWC
- 1 time finalist Entrepreneur of the Year Southern California Technology Council

Pricing Your Practice

- Guest speaker at over 100 elementary schools statewide (sponsored by Verizon on behalf of the California PTA) for Poogling Internet Safety and Information Seminars

- Various other schools, colleges, universities and organizations: Regular speaker on Entrepreneuring, Marketing, PR, Extreme Customer Service, management, and other topics.

OBJECTIVE

To do cool stuff, solve problems, make a difference, matter, and have tons of fun doing it working only with amazing people, who want to do the same.

EXPERIENCE

2018 – current: Founder, Chairman of the Board, Mud Angels, Inc. a 501c3 non profit corporation

On January 9, 2018 "Mud Angels" began appearing everywhere. They were ordinary people that did extraordinary things. The movement arose in response to the Thomas Fire induced mud flow that destroyed 300 homes in Montecito in the middle of the night, consuming everything and everyone in its path. 23 souls were lost and thousands suffered massive loss of personal property, business revenue, loved ones and peace of mind. The less impacted Montecito residents and neighbors grew wings and took action. They helped sort through the mud to find lost treasures, dug the mud out of homes and yards, raised hundreds of thousands of financial aid, provided housing, transportation, food and so much more.

The Mud Angels organization was created to help others organize their support, help victims with financial support, and honor and thank other Mud Angels. It's also a place for remembering those lost and missing, recognition of donors, showcase lost / found items, links to local shops, and gratitude for our first responders and emergency personnel, along with countless others. Visit mudangels.com.

2010 – current: Founder, Chief Clever Officer, 74 Degrees LLC / 74 Systems

74 Systems provides cutting edge marketing, technology and automation services for professional services companies and individuals. We help you Ignite your practice or business through branding, client acquisition,

business development, business structure, pricing, packaging, technology, automation, and everything else you need to grow a business, revenues and profits. The IGNITE Program has helped countless entrepreneurs and business owners jumpstart or expand their practices/businesses. We help business owners ignite, acquire customers and increase revenue. Then, we help them facilitate the processes needed to keep their clients happy.

74 Degrees LLC also built and operates schoolofbookkeeping.com.

2001 – 2012: Founder, CEO, Make It Work, Inc.

Make It Work® was formed in 2001 to satisfy the need of the fast growing consumer electronics sector. With a focus on extreme customer service, the company grew and doubled in size each of its first 5 years. It's fleet of red and white Mini Coopers became an iconic part of Southern California freeways.

Major accomplishments in marketing and customer acquisition:

- Acquired over 40,000 customers and over 44,000 customer testimonials.
- Raised over $4 million in equity.
- Purchased/leased over 135 Mini Coopers.
- In 2008, The company structured a one of a kind deal with Verizon Communications. The company became the first partner in history to be referred by Verizon field technicians.
- In 2009, we created Tech News, powered by Make It Work which aired every Saturday, 1pm on CBS Radio's KNX 1070 in Los Angeles through February of 2011. In January of 2010, we launched Make It Work which aired every Saturday, 3pm on ABC/Citadel Radio's KSFO 560 in San Francisco through February of 2011.

In 2011, my team and I launched its offering inside of 20 Costco stores. In May of 2012, the company began planning for deploying to all locations via Costco.com.

Here are a few of our other achievements:

Pricing Your Practice

- The company was named Software Services Company of the Year by the Software Council of Southern California.

- The company has been named "Best Of" in computer repair by the Santa Barbara Independent twice.

- It was named 4th Fastest Growing Company in the Tri-counties by Pacific Coast Business Times and Best Place to Work.

- The company made the Inc 500 list in 2007 as the 78th fastest growing IT company in the United States.

- The company created Poogling Internet Safety Seminars for parents of kids in elementary and middle school.

- Eric is also a recipient of the prestigious 40 under 40 award from the same publication.

- 1999 – 2001: Co-founder/CEO/CMO, Push, Inc.

In September of 1999, I sold my former company and was asked to join the new company as CEO. I helped create one of the highest profile Application Service Providers in the industry, the predecessor to SAAS and cloud computing. While at Push, my focus and dedication was on sales, business development and strategy. As part of an amazing team, I successfully negotiated an equity transaction with KPMG worth 20% of the Company. In addition, my team and I secured a contract with KPMG worth $5.5 million, one of the largest in the industry. I managed the team, building a carrier class datacenter valued at over $10 million and established a partnership with KPMG for branding, distribution, and marketing. As the head of sales, I helped make Push the #1 ASP for sales force automation according to PC/ Magazine and #1 hosting partner for SalesLogix (Interact Commerce, now owned by Sage, PLC) by both revenue and seat count. I also helped lead Push to become Microsoft's #3 revenue producer, a leading and founding partner of Sprint's Enabling ASP program, a member of Hewlett Packard's Channels on Tap program, a member of the distinguished Board of Governors for Citrix Systems' iBusiness iCouncil, and an executive member of the ASP Industry Consortium. During his tenure at Push, I was profiled on the cover of Windows2000 Magazine, various press releases from Sprint, Hewlett Packard, and Citrix, various feature articles in the Santa Barbara

Eric Greenspan

News Press, Tech Republic, ERP Supersite, Netopia, Newsedge, Netscape News, CNET, ASP Street, Yahoo, Morningstar, HRIMMALL, The Street, Webharbor, ASPNews.com, Thin Planet, ASP Island, SAM Magazine. The company was also profiled in various case studies by Citrix, SalesLogix and Hewlett Packard. In April of 2001, I sold my interest in the Company.

- Assisted Chairman in the raising of ~$10,000,000 in financing much from an equity investment from KPMG, LLP;

- Negotiated and closed a $6 million contract with KPMG LLP for over 1000 seats;

- Negotiated a distribution agreement with KPMG to sell directly into their channels leveraging their brand and client base;

- Became the #1 Sales Force Automation ASP (according to PC/ Magazine);

- Built, managed and motivated a highly successful sales team;

- Designed and implemented many high profile, very successful marketing campaigns;

- Named a member of the Board of Governors for the iBusiness Program by Citrix Systems, 1 of 4 companies of a pool of over 125. Responsibilities included advising Citrix C level executives on burgeoning new industry;

- Sat on numerous panels, featured on the cover of Windows2000 Magazine and have spoken at numerous industry conferences.

1995 – 1999: Founder/CEO/CMO, Make It Work, Inc. (first generation)

Make It Work designed, built and supported local area networks on Windows servers. The company was considered innovative as Novell was the leading software for such implementations during this period. Make It Work also designed and managed custom software projects for customer relationship management and accounting. Make It Work's custom software solutions soon would become a major revenue generator and focus for the company.

Make It Work began to expand its offerings and skill set by embracing server based computing. Partnered with Citrix and Microsoft, Make It Work began installing and maintaining Citrix WinFrame/MetaFrame solutions for centralized deployment of applications to any device, over any connection, available anywhere in the world.

In its final year, Make It Work became the 42nd Citrix PLATINUM partner, awarded to only 42 out of 8800 partners. As a Platinum partner, our relationships with Citrix grew and we worked directly with their executive team, including CEO and Senior Vice Presidents of all product lines and services.

Began as a one man technician and programmer and grew the business fast;

Due to levels of enterprise sales, MIW became the #1 Citrix reseller in Central California, achieving Platinum status afforded to only a handful of Citrix partners worldwide (only 42 firms of 8000);

Created and directed Thindex, a leading server-based computing seminar event educating the IT community on thin client and server based computing with partners such as Citrix, Microsoft, HP, Symantec and IBM;

The business was accepted to Garage.com in 1999 and sold weeks later.

1992 – 1995: Senior Vice President, CMO, Investors Rights Association

Technical consulting, client management system development;

Advised clients, assisted in case preparation.

I was hired by IRA to assist in the filing of over 250 cases stacked in banker's boxes in the company's offices. I built a Microsoft Access database that allowed each case to be managed for filing deadlines, mail merge, and customer relationship management. In 30 days, all 250 cases were ready for filing and were successfully submitted to the National Association of Securities Dealers and the American Arbitration Association.

I continued to expand and manage the custom software as the company grew. Once the application was in full production, I began to build out tools that could be used for research and case development, as well as presentation tools for hearings. Using a laptop and a LCD projector (state of the art at that time), I began working with the attorneys and experts to build an electronic case presentation system, illustrating the facts using images, video, statistics, charts and graphs. This led to presentation development for seminars and customer meetings.

1989 – 1992: Education Marketing Representative, IBM Corporation

Developed and managed student, faculty and staff sales programs throughout Central Coast colleges and universities including: UCSB, Santa Barbara City College, Westmont College, Cal Lutheran, and Cal Poly, SLO;

Achieved record sales for my territory;

Was offered several top positions with IBM prior to my departure;

One of the youngest IBMers in history.

I was hired by IBM to build and manage the sales program for colleges and universities on the Central Coast of California, including: UCSB, Cal Poly, SLO, Cal Lutheran, Santa Barbara City College, Westmont College and others. I recruited the sales team, managed day to day activities, established a marketing budget, held sales seminars at the campuses and continued to successfully grow the sales for the program.

During this time, IBM was going through its largest layoff period in history and I was one of only 4 remaining (of 144) IBMers at the Santa Barbara office before it closed in 1995. I was offered a variety of positions with IBM in their Los Angeles office, but declined to complete my degree.

EDUCATION

1991 – 1995: University of California, Santa Barbara

B.A*., Law and Society (Political Science) *lacking a lower division course, thanks IBM

(Worked as an IBM Education Marketing Representative, full time)

1987 – 1991: Santa Barbara City College

A.A.

IBM Internship

Pricing Your Practice

Transferred to UCSB

1986 – 1987: Kent State University

SPECIAL TALENTS

I'm a dad of two gorgeous boys. I love the kitchen. I'm also an accomplished public speaker, a motivator, and have the ability to make decisions and think on my feet in an extraordinary capacity. I'm a total geek, and I know as much about technology as Gretzky knows hockey. I am well-versed and highly experienced in enterprise relationship building, funding, legal, financial planning and modeling, and marketing. My passion runs deep for anything I'm involved in. I believe in 100% dedication, focus and pure integrity to shareholders, employees, family and friends. I have and understand the balance necessary in life to ensure success and happiness. I'm also a TEDster, an avid fan of sushi, anything on Food Network after 5pm, and world travel.

CHAPTER THIRTEEN
The "Close"

Until We Meet Again

I wrote this book to help people understand, create and manage pricing. I'm not sure if it's going to be a big hit or not, and honestly I'm not concerned about that. I wrote this book because it was a goal I set for myself. I'm now finished with it and it's published on Amazon. My sales in the first two days put us at #1 in Business Accounting and #47 in Business and Money. Not too shabby for a first time author. But as I said, it's not about this. Well, maybe a little because my confidence is lifted right now. I feel proud, accomplished and no matter the results of my book sales, the benefits of writing this book will outweigh any potential income directly. That said, my next book might make me a fortune, but what I'm really hoping for is that thousands read it and successfully grow their practice. That won't be bad for my consulting business. I love these types of win wins.

Thanks for taking the time to read my book. Drop me a note to eric@74systems.com to say hello and let me know your thoughts or visit 74systems.com/start if you need some one on one help. We love meeting new people.

Made in the USA
Columbia, SC
18 September 2019